SAY PARDON

Say Pardon

By DAVID IGNATOW

WESLEYAN UNIVERSITY PRESS
Middletown, Connecticut

Certain of these poems have previously appeared elsewhere. Grateful
acknowledgments are due to the following: *American Poetry Magazine,
Beloit Poetry Journal, Between Worlds, Botteghe Oscure, The Chelsea,
Chicago Jewish Forum, Commentary, The Fifties, Midstream, The Na-
tion, New Orleans Poetry Journal, New World Writing* (May 1957),
Poetry, Saturday Review, The Village Voice, Voices.

Library of Congress Catalog Card Number: 61-6973
Manufactured in the United States of America
First printing February 1961; second printing April 1968

To W. C. Williams and Rose Graubart

Contents

SECTION ONE

How Come?

I'm in New York covered by a layer of soap foam.
The air is dense from the top of skyscrapers
to the sidewalk in every street, avenue
and alley, as far as Babylon on the East,
Dobbs Ferry on the North, Coney Island
on the South and stretching far over
the Atlantic Ocean. I wade
through, breathing by pushing
foam aside. The going is slow,
with just a clearing ahead
by swinging my arms. Others are groping
from all sides, too. We keep moving.
Everything else has happened here
and we've survived: snow storms,
traffic tieups, train breakdowns, bursting
water mains; and now I am writing
with a lump of charcoal stuck between my toes,
switching it from one foot to the other—
this monkey trick learned visiting
with my children at the zoo of a Sunday.
But soap foam filling the air,
the bitter, fatty smell of it . . . How come?
My portable says it extends to San Francisco!
Listen to this, and down to the Mexican border
and as far north as Canada. All the prairies,
the Rocky Mountains, the Great Lakes, Chicago,
the Pacific Coast. No advertising stunt
could do this. The soap has welled out of the ground
says the portable suddenly. The scientists report
the soil saturated. And now what?

We'll have to start climbing for air,
a crowd forming around the Empire State Building
says the portable. God help the many
who will die of soap foam.

The News Photo

This idiot had suffered his own faults,
but since it was this country
and he had done a thing beyond himself,
by the axe, and since it was an act
that could be called public,
in the interest of the public to be known,
he was to be shown in this act,
in its way instructive: they had been his parents
and he had tried not to,
shouting at them to beware, as they slept;
he had wept, and since in this manner
he had cleansed himself,
he could grin for his picture.

Doctor

The patient cries, Give me back feeling.
And the doctor studies the books:
what injection is suitable for hysterics,
syndrome for insecurity, hallucination?
The patient cries, I have been disinherited.
The doctor studies the latest bulletins
of the Psychiatric Institute and advises
one warm bath given at the moment of panic.
Afterwards inject a barbiturate. At this
the patient rises up from bed and slugs
the doctor and puts him unconscious to bed;
and himself reads the book through the night
avidly without pause.

Obsolete

I'm going to drive up
to the gate and tell him
to take the knock out
of the motor and the bump
out of the spring
and straighten the bent-in side,
repaint the body
and put in new upholstery.
I'll pay him a fair price.
I've sat behind this wheel
ten years. I don't need
a new car, I just need
repairs. This fellow
will blow up, he'll go mad,
he'll want to beat me,
his eyes bloodshot, his voice
thick to know if I'm a wise guy,
with him standing
in front of his new cars
and if he pulls me out
and beats me, I'll know
damn well he's admitting
he can't make me obsolete.

Side by Side

What does it mean to be mature?
We have got to take hold of the fellow
we work with and whom we trust to be true
to us in a crisis and say to him,
gripping him by the shirt front
near the throat, our face thrust into his:
snarl at him, "Now look here, I see clear
through you, playing me for a sucker
by being nice to me. You want to get away
with something without paying for it.
I am not going to let you, see?
I am not going to be taken advantage of,
and when I get the chance to do what I want
I shall do it with much more ruthlessness
than you and not be tied up in feelings.
After that I shall be friends with you,
once I have what I want from you."
This being maturity, I turn to him
as we sit side by side working
and say aloud so that it may be heard
all over, "Give me a cigarette, will you,
I'm all out of them."

Shined Shoes

Get a shine. Who knows, it might lead to money.
Somebody seeing you well groomed, thinking
this man has no real need, will approach
and say, I have money for you.
At this point, overcome by pride
I will respond, I have plenty of my own,
at which he will know, since there is no end
to the need, that like so many with shined shoes,
I live on a budget.

The Golden Calf

Before the sacrifice the animal is fed.
They let him roam the streets, and find
a mate for him. He drinks their wine
and fills himself on love. They lead
him to the altar past the sights enjoyed,
the standing towers, the tall women
who mothered him. They gave their milk
and promised happiness. A golden ring
set in his nose, he trots benignly
to his death.

        The women stamp
their merriment, the men approve.
Spilled blood will make the grapes
grow large, and if that fails
they'll set another offering
and still more, a worshiped sacrifice,
till all the joys they feed it
fall to them. He trots benignly
to his death.

Mr. Mammon 1

It was no use their pleading with me
to whom they came for pay Fridays.
I demanded loyalty, efficiency,
promptness and no problem about it.
I would raise my voice too in anger
or sarcasm and I would see white
come into their faces. At these moments
one would walk out the door
and not return. I'd have to mail
the final check. The others
would go about their work dazed-looking.
I'd be sorry but I'd be practical too,
entering my office and shutting the door
behind me. I was no dream of human perfection,
nor did I intend that in business.
Miserable as they were the most part of the week,
holidays would have them pray for perfect mercy,
which left me to feel an outsider,
and I did not pray, standing in Our Lord's presence
for judgment, as I felt myself
each day of the week.

Mr. Mammon II

In business my ideal is to get up
to adjust a screw or a bill
or a customer's complaint,
taking in all about ten minutes;
then to retire hands in pockets
to my office and stand looking
out the window at traffic
and to hear the machines go
inside the shop and to feel
I am lending my presence.
I would have a relationship to God
to think about. I would feel
His presence, along with unease
at my freedom, and I would imagine
this condition something to bear
gracefully, requiring just this
idleness. And I would remove
my hands from my pockets
and return to the shop
and stroll its length and width,
looking over my machines and help,
in pity and humiliation.
I would know what it means
to betray, to invite betrayal.
And I would reply, Oh Lord,
why did you give me this desire
for freedom, if not to feel
myself in your presence?

The Errand Boy I

To get quicker through the day
and to bring on night as a blessing,
to lie down in a sleep that is a dream
of completion, he takes up his package
from the floor—he has been ordered
to do so, heavy as it is, his knees weakening
as he walks, one would never know
by his long stride—and carries it
to the other end of the room.

The Errand Boy II

It was the way he went to pick up the carton
fallen to the gutter from his handtruck,
his arms outstretched, his body stooping
to the ground. I wondered at the smile,
weary and amused and so gentle withal,
as if this was what he had expected,
not for the first time and not
for the last time either.

14

The Manager

I want no balking, no hesitation
as to my meaning, not even
at the slightest pressure
of my thumb, and I will not feel
miserable about it. I will have nothing
rub me the wrong way, I will have everything
my way and the result will be
that I will not know which way
is which, with everything giving in
at a look; and think,
I'll not have anger to bear
any longer, I'll be happy dead.

The Professional

She has begun to see men invite themselves.
The flowers and fruit and other gifts pile up.
She wonders, if only she could turn all that
back into cash, how well off she could be.
She must first have had a pride in her abilities.

One man, any, all, each a new subtlety
and overtone that goes to prove an idea
and work supporting it, of which she honestly
has become proud; to be able at a glance
to tell what any amateur would need seclusion for
and a dim light. She has all that
at her fingertips now—starting
from a sincere liking for that kind of knowledge.

Adroit now and live to technique,
she is quick to tell you her main interest
in tones that hardly hurt,
they are so direct and clear—
no longer hers, but of a spirit that demands
to be compensated for its skill.

On Being Practical

—then figure your death
by the cost of the coffin,
the size of the funeral procession
and the price of the preacher,
and feel if your heart does not skip
in plain dread, half dead already
at the idea of the coffin,
the paid preacher, the hired cars,
your best friends, your lovers
for whom you strove in the morning
and in the evening to please
and be pleased by with working
at trucking, mailing, teaching others
a new idea. Did they return your smile
in the evening at the door
opened by you—the coffin,
the hired preacher or the funeral car?

The Paper Cutter

He slides the cut paper out
from under the raised knife.
His face does not lose interest.
"And now I go to my night job,"
he says cheerfully at five,
wiping his hands upon a rag.
He has stood all day in one spot,
pressing first the left
and then the right button.
"And what are you going to do
with all that money?" I ask.
His shoulders stick out bony.
"I will buy a house
and then I will lie down in it
and not get up all day," he laughs.

The Dream

Someone approaches to say his life is ruined
and to fall down at your feet
and pound his head upon the sidewalk.
Blood spreads in a puddle.
And you, in a weak voice, plead
with those nearby for help;
your life takes on his desperation.
He keeps pounding his head.
It is you who are fated;
and you fall down beside him.
It is then you are awakened,
the body gone, the blood washed from the ground,
the stores lit up with their goods.

The Transcendentalist Walking
Through Skid Row

He is in the secret
though he could not tell you
for money or for truth its substance,
which is the way of a man
who can tell himself his good fortune
and his desires were vague.
He allows himself neither shame nor terror,
and he is gone to his business
off the street of sprawled men
before they can sit up to talk to him.
He will be justified in his preoccupation.
He presumes much.
It is a happy thought.

Night People

See them with their backs
to the sun, studying their shadows
long and dark, and none thinks
to turn around. It will be night
and they will begin to move
among themselves silently,
touching each other for signposts.
No one will speak
and no arm be raised
in a gesture, as they vanish.

Each Night

I see a flat hat upon the river;
beneath it, I imagine, my cousin,
face rigid with thought, eyes closed
the better to see; and still, still
as a monument for the sound.

He was an artist, faces caught
within a frame by shadow; desiring light
only, they gazed fixedly out.

   .   .   .   .   .

In your tenement, soiled shades
of the poor, your brush lies idle,
while from the rain-blotched wall
hangs the burlesque of a millionaire.
I could not believe in it, Al;
each stroke deliberately crude but caricatured
your sadness: your mother's breasts and belly
bleary and drawn: her voice instructing you
in the sounds of the world—full of complaint;
your father's reply rough, and dead
in its decisiveness. He could not be budged,
curt as the limits he had set.
All this was your legitimate complaint.

Float away from me, my kin; my grief
and sinking sigh the waves and the trough
carrying you, touching and withdrawing
and touching once more to find you dead.

   .   .   .   .   .

But each night, crossing the bridge from work,
I look for you, tiny light refractions
from my train dot and dash signals upon the waves,

"Come out." See, each morning I ride willingly,
and at night compose poems to tiredness
and disillusion, and to hope pinnacled
upon receding towers. I too emerged
from a hardening womb: choked arteries,
stalled vehicles belching frustration,
where bums lie sprawled, toxic with fumes—
and children white with wanting
upon the narrow causeways. My parents
were the city and its complaint of brakes
and horns. For food I sucked at exhaust pipes,
and heard overhead rumbling motor of argument,
playing in my mother's lap, the gutter.
Now grown, drunk and staggering from my repast,
I travel between home and hell, always
with a pencil, to punch holes for air
when breathing becomes difficult.

Each night, crossing the bridge, train lights
appeal to you, Take back your brush,
Oh reach for it from the river.

Say Pardon

Say pardon to a bum,
brushing past him.
He could lean back
and spit
and you would have to wipe it off.
How would you explain
that you have insulted
this man's identity,
of his own choosing;
and others could only scratch
their heads and advise you
to move on
and be quiet.
Say pardon
and follow your own will
in the open spaces ahead.

There Is the Law

There is the law,
the extent of my pride.
Beyond stands the transgressor.
I turn to the calming law,
and my death will come as providentially,
my faults codified.
I will die in the law,
with you who abide.

My Pity

This locked man,
a springer of death upon himself,
shut face. His look is killing,
I am deprived of my pity.
There is motion,
he has crossed a leg,
his agony embodied.
I know, for I withdraw myself
from its sight,
my pity back again.

The Complex

My father's madness is to own himself,
for what he gives is taken. He is
a single son of God. He is mad
to know the loves he owns are for his keeping,
so if he does not love he is without himself,
for God has said, Of love you are a man.
You are yourself, apart from me.
And madly my father seeks his loves,
with whom there is no standing,
for as he would own himself
he is the measuring rod,
and slowly owes himself to God,
giving of himself with forced breath.

In Limbo

I have a child in limbo
I must bring back.
My experience grows
but there is no wisdom
without a child in the house.

Sunday at the State Hospital

I am sitting across the table
eating my visit sandwich.
The one I brought him stays suspended
near his mouth; his eyes focus
on the table and seem to think,
his shoulders hunched forward.
I chew methodically,
pretending to take him
as a matter of course.
The sandwich tastes mad
and I keep chewing.
My past is sitting in front of me
filled with itself
and trying with almost no success
to bring the present to its mouth.

29

Mother and Child

She feared the baby would fall.
Upside down she held it.
She loved her child.
As a born baby, it was a practical thing,
handled by doctors. As a drowned baby,
it still would exist.

By accident it died inside its tub.
She carried it carefully to its crib
and there rocked it, as she called for help.
Help, help, she called.
Help, help, she whispered,
hands resting upon her.

Walt Whitman in the
Civil War Hospitals

Prescient, my hands soothing
their foreheads, by my love
I earn them. In their presence
I am wretched as death. They smile
to me of love. They cheer me
and I smile. These are stones
in the catapulting world;
they fly, bury themselves in flesh,
in a wall, in earth; in midair
break against each other
and are without sound.
I sent them catapulting.
They outflew my voice
towards vacant spaces,
but I have called them farther,
to the stillness beyond,
to death which I have praised.

SECTION TWO

My Only Enemy

My only enemy has no metal for his hatred,
it comes invisible;
and if I were not indisposed
you would not know I am attacked.
I will die but not at his doing.
It will take my aging friends,
the moon and stars; they are my laughter.
In their light I am disarmed,
sterile to their intelligence.
That is me,
that is how I'll die.
I do not forget my only enemy.

The Orange Picker

I was tempted to the grove by its odor;
the tang lingered over the whole countryside,
and from the hilltop where I stood orange
was the banner laid out like a signal.
I had no exact notion, but of itself
it seemed a goal: to be overwhelmed
in its odor.
        I came downhill,
and saw these men at work,
on ladders to pick oranges;
they were not tall enough;
and as I watched I too was drawn in.
And now as I labor, the days going by redolent—
I have breathed in them too long to be curious—
these oranges have failed me.

Self-Centered

I love the only day that I was born,
as if in my oneness I could love another,
and yet I love a day. As of the beginning
I am here, but have come really
from the second day in which a sky was made.
Before everything I was what I do not know,
an absence, a beginning. There has been none
since the start. Therefore to love my only day
is to be set apart,
and this what I do when I am one,
and there is what has been,
at which time I was the beginning.

Guilt

Guilt is my one attachment to reality,
for having failed at so much
that now when I refer myself to those failures
I consider life to be formed on these terms;
so that when I am joyful at all I know
for sure that somewhere I have strayed.
My joys are infinite and give my faults
their power to rule me at the end so strongly,
I fly so high and far, that when I am returned
it is to feel that as far as I have flown
that too is the extent of my fault.

Be Like Me

I will walk, if I must,
in a crowd, so that I am kind.
I cannot think, as if I had lost
something that love comes from.
I do not even know
to whom I am talking.
I break off and try to revise.
Someone comes by and whispers,
"Be like me."

A Man

A man confronted by masks
begins to maneuver
out of their reach.
With satisfaction
he sees one fall
as if it had been struck;
it lies crumpled.
He hears weeping,
someone loved
is now a cause for tears.

Joseph

Joseph saw no trouble ahead,
he had his father's backing.
He went about smiling and nodding
at others—wherein their reservations
lay, and once too often
he nodded and smiled
at his brothers.

        He was wiser
years later, angry but ashamed.
Seated on a throne,
to hide his troubled thoughts
he made his brothers tremble
for their lives.

The Prodigal Son

I went back for redress,
I would show my father
how much better I could act
in his place, and when I had bound
myself to his circumstance
I found my only satisfaction
in setting him
adrift.

The Pariah

In the beginning
I expect an evil response
and I will shield myself
in pride. There will be
some to forgive and to regret
my outspokenness
and to qualify their judgement,
sensing I would have said
something of the worth
in each of us,
but that I was inhibited
as one who was alone
in his thoughts.

The Escapade

Poet and gangster reach in the dark;
blind flashes reveal them.
The dead collapse and the living scatter
for cover. Alone now, they think the street
is theirs and swiftly they make their getaway,
in the left hand the haul, in the right
jammed in the driver's back the weapon
as they careen; and at the hideout set up
to repel the law—coming nearly as swift
sirening. In the inferno, started by both sides,
riddled, still seeking to shoot,
they sink to their deaths,
the haul beside them still theirs.

44

And Step

I understand myself
in relation to a stone,
flesh and bone.
Shall I bow down
to stone? Mine
is the voice
I hear. I will
stand up to stone.
I will be proud
and fragile, I will
be personable
and step over
stone.

I Stand Upon a Dike

I stand upon a dike at night, watching
over the sea's extreme edge sparse settled lights
snap like traffic signals. The ocean
is a darkened ballroom lacking the Saturday night crowd;
the place is sad.

Below me a wave out of the darkness
rushes through a pile of rocks
and sucks them down. Where is the ocean,
the strength of the wave? I see only foam,
white raving, white eyes of nothing.

The wave recedes into the dark for its impetus;
it lashes out from a silent poise,
it sucks down the rocks, hurls spray at me.
It makes me crouch; I cannot shame it,
it has no eyes nor ears.
I cannot die victorious from its beating,
it has no argument.
It races out of the dark knowing nothing,
and I have only this dike.

Content

I should be content
to look at a mountain
for what it is
and not as a comment
on my life.

The Good Angel

Time and again he would come
to give his impossible conditions.
I'd shrug. He'd plead, command,
Do as I say and I will lead your life;
you will float on that shining cloud.
I will do it because I love you,
you are pitiful. And I'd look at him.
Those conditions he would impose on me—
I'd tell him bitterly about them.
He'd try to explain. He was to be won
under those terms, as he understood himself.
I'd continue on my hopeless way,
from home to work and back.
I would see men carefree and fresh
and I'd know they had done the impossible.
At home I found him under my dining table,
asleep and snoring in careless disregard.
I was angry. How could he taunt me,
dying for his favors? I kicked him
and he sprang up and flung his arms apart
and said, At last!

48

Blessing Myself

I believe in stillness,
I close a door
and surrender myself
to a wall and converse
with it and ask it
to bless me.
The wall is silent.
I speak for it,
blessing myself.

Awaiting

A man with head lifted stands listening
for a sound in an empty field.
He thinks he hears a voice
and is straining to make out
what it is saying.
It is no hallucination
and he stands awaiting
clarification.

All Comes

All comes to sunlight.
A bird stirring its wings.
In the air it has the shape of a dream.
It too is perfect off the ground,
I follow its flight.

Whistle or Hoot

The bird that sings to itself
is never a lonely or frightened bird;
though if before it were silent,
darting its head for worms
or worrisome matters,
now that it sings to itself
it triumphs, whistle or hoot.

Like a Lie

In myself I speak the language of love
and to the outside, of practical matters
because I do not wish to make the truth
sound like a lie.

No Answer

I have learned to love without explanation
for even as I kneel
under a dreadful claw
I yet have the ease
without which I can expect
no answer.

Everybody Knows

The flowers we forget to buy
on birthdays, so busy with everything—
we retrace our steps to say something
apologetic.
      And the flowers we do buy;
everybody knows what flowers cost.

Brief Elegy

In every beautiful song is a promise of sleep.
I will sleep if you will sing to me,
but sing to me of sleep
when the bells have hushed in the towers
and the towers have hushed from their sounds.
Sing to me, strolling through silent streets.

This Is Mortal

The lit room is blinding.
We are moments of the heart.
There is a silence between beats,
no beat for the same blood twice.
We love one another like the motion
of the blood, and there is no outcry,
for this is mortal
in the bright room.

With the Door Open

Something I want to communicate to you,
I keep my door open between us.
I am unable to say it,
I am happy only
with the door open between us.

The Lover

I'd tell of stones dropping upon me
from a high mountain, but to leave
is to lose a mountain and to stay
is to cry, Let me go away.
I would know if you were to stop
suddenly from hurling your stones
and remained perfectly still and cold
in my presence. Then I would leave
humiliated, seeking for something
to be aware of me, even in anger,
as you are. But such anger—
why am I made aware of it
and why does it prolong its torture of me
if its purpose is to be rid of me?
That question keeps me rooted
beneath your height on which I see the sun
dazzle my eyes, as though everything
were well and behovely.

Apple Watcher

Rose is my apple watcher
sitting in a tree
and I watch Rose
counting apples
she believes in.
She smiles the whole crop in
and the one she throws me
as the best I believe
even if it will not chew
because I too am smiled in,
just like you,
old battered skin.

SECTION THREE

The Mountain Is Stripped

I no longer have to declare myself;
a quietness urges me, regardless
of my grievance, to go about.
I affect the justice of my cause;
while I live I am the answer to harm.

I have been made frail with righteousness:
with two voices. I am but one person.
The warning voice is God:
the whales are bled in the sea,
the mountain is stripped.

I Felt

I felt I had met the Lord.
He calmed me, calling me
to look into my child's room.
He said, I am love,
and you will win your life
out of my hands
by taking up your child.

Without Fear

I weep to myself
and I ask if this self-pity,
terror and love are not enough
to preserve us, and I think
then that all will be well.
Without fear of contradiction,
I give you God in my life.

And I Stand

Behind my enemy stands God,
watching how near I come
to killing, to making
my own world and time,
and then ask His love.
And I stand and gaze
past my enemy at Him.

I Shall Follow

I shall follow
as the shadow that has mountains
in its path. You are undeformed
by these imperceptions, and I shall not be
constrained either in pursuit,
attached to you as an emanation is.
This is how I shall complete my happiness,
in you.

For the Living

Said the Lord, I am humble
of my powers and you
who are proud I will let live
as long as my humility abides
which is forever—
but I have proclaimed judgment
against you.

He Puts Me to Rest

I am unhappy that I am not God,
I talk to myself and listen,
hoping to find in this dialogue
a hint of Him. I do things
and measure them to find
God there, or, if not,
that this would prove
the opposite is true.
I would do this opposite
to become God. I think of it,
and when I must sleep
He puts me to rest.

In Your Dreams

If life is to be sand and salt
what is the power that moves me to complain?
The withheld sweetness that I can surmise
from pain?

       Pluck out the root
of planted bitter herb, sunk in my love
for you, sweet source. You are the soil
of my distress, to bid me live.
God, in your desires, seek a child
in your dreams.

Noah

He must wade out to a high point
and build an ark of the trees,
take two of each kind of happiness.
And send out
a pigeon that shall not return,
after the bubbling shriek of the drowned;
it shall land upon a rock.
God of his crying shall have made the flood subside.
He shall emerge
upon the earth, brown for grief
of its dead, and know no better
than before, save there is a promise
to cling to when the floods rise.

God Said

God said, Have you finished my thinking?
Now think yourself into stone
and I will lift you
and set you upon a mountain.

Samson

Did I love God for myself alone
or for my enemies' sake also
that I might not despair of God's goodness?
With the jawbone of an ass
I had killed contemptuously.
I loved Delilah and I would teach her
His love that she might go and speak
to them in earnest and she did speak
and I pulled the pillars down
one by one in bitter surprise
that goodness could give my enemy
triumph.

A Semblance

Over your mother's grave
speak a prayer of bafflement,
grasp the hand of the rabbi,
nearest to steady you.
He recites the prayer
for you to follow unsteadily
its meaning. You pray
to the air.

Job's Anger

It was not a man's way to plead
with God. Strength and will
had built his house. He would
bring God down and he cursed
and challenged God
to make Himself known
and to defend Himself
from Job's anger
that strength and will
were not enough,
and God came down.

The Rightful One

I heard my son burst out of his room
and shout, He is here, dad. He is here.
I understood and I managed to stand up,
melting within, and walk the hall
between our rooms to meet Him
whom I had neglected in my thoughts;
but not my son who was ill
and had searched for Him.
He had come. I saw Him standing,
his hair long, face exhausted, eyes sad
and knowing, and I bent my knee,
terrified at the reality,
but he restrained me with a hand
and said, I am a sufferer like yourself.
I have come to let you know.
And I arose, my heart swelling, and said,
I have failed and bitterness is in me.
And he replied, And forgiveness too.
Bless your son. And I blessed him
and his face brightened. And the Rightful One
was gone and left a power to feel free.

Distinguished contemporary poetry in cloth and paperback editions

ALAN ANSEN: *Disorderly Houses* (1961)

JOHN ASHBERY: *The Tennis Court Oath* (1962)

ROBERT BAGG: *Madonna of the Cello* (1961)

ROBERT BLY: *Silence in the Snowy Fields* (1962)

TURNER CASSITY: *Watchboy, What of the Night?* (1966)

TRAM COMBS: *saint thomas. poems.* (1965)

DONALD DAVIE: *Events and Wisdoms* (1965); *New and Selected Poems* (1961)

JAMES DICKEY: *Buckdancer's Choice* (1965) [National Book Award in Poetry, 1966]; *Drowning With Others* (1962); *Helmets* (1964)

DAVID FERRY: *On the Way to the Island* (1960)

ROBERT FRANCIS: *The Orb Weaver* (1960)

JOHN HAINES: *Winter News* (1966)

RICHARD HOWARD: *The Damages* (1967); *Quantities* (1962)

BARBARA HOWES: *Light and Dark* (1959)

DAVID IGNATOW: *Figures of the Human* (1964); *Rescue the Dead* (1968); *Say Pardon* (1961)

DONALD JUSTICE: *Night Light* (1967); *The Summer Anniversaries* (1960) [A Lamont Poetry Selection]

CHESTER KALLMAN: *Absent and Present* (1963)

PHILIP LEVINE: *Not This Pig* (1968)

LOU LIPSITZ: *Cold Water* (1967)

JOSEPHINE MILES: *Kinds of Affection* (1967)

VASSAR MILLER: *My Bones Being Wiser* (1963); *Wage War on Silence* (1960)

W. R. MOSES: *Identities* (1965)

DONALD PETERSEN: *The Spectral Boy* (1964)

MARGE PIERCY: *Breaking Camp* (1968)

HYAM PLUTZIK: *Apples from Shinar* (1959)

VERN RUTSALA: *The Window* (1964)

HARVEY SHAPIRO: *Battle Report* (1966)

JON SILKIN: *Poems New and Selected* (1966)

LOUIS SIMPSON: *At the End of the Open Road* (1963) [Pulitzer Prize in Poetry, 1964]; *A Dream of Governors* (1959)

JAMES WRIGHT: *The Branch Will Not Break* (1963); *Saint Judas* (1959)